This book is dedicated to
Emma, Lydia, Darly, and Domnica —
May they find careers that fulfill
their dreams and imagination.

Henry Holt and Company, LLC
Publishers since 1866
175 Fifth Avenue
New York, New York 10010
www.HenryHoltKids.com

Henry Holt® is a registered trademark of Henry Holt and Company, LLC.
Copyright © 2008 by Jessica Loy
All rights reserved.
Distributed in Canada by H. B. Fenn and Company Ltd.

Photo credits: pp. 12–13, artifact photos courtesy of the New York State Museum in Albany;
p. 23, photo of newly installed play station by Katherine M. Quimby; p. 33,
set photos for *Peter Pan*, *A Tale of Cinderella*, *The Wizard of Oz*, and *Man of La Mancha*
provided by Richard Finkelstein; p. 31, contact sheet images by Kim Levin;
unless otherwise noted, all other photos were taken by Jessica Loy.

Library of Congress Catalog Card Number: 2007938930
ISBN-13: 978-0-8050-7717-9
ISBN-10: 0-8050-7717-0

First Edition—2008
The artist used computer-generated illustrations and photography
to create the images for this book.
Printed in China on acid-free paper. ∞

1   3   5   7   9   10   8   6   4   2

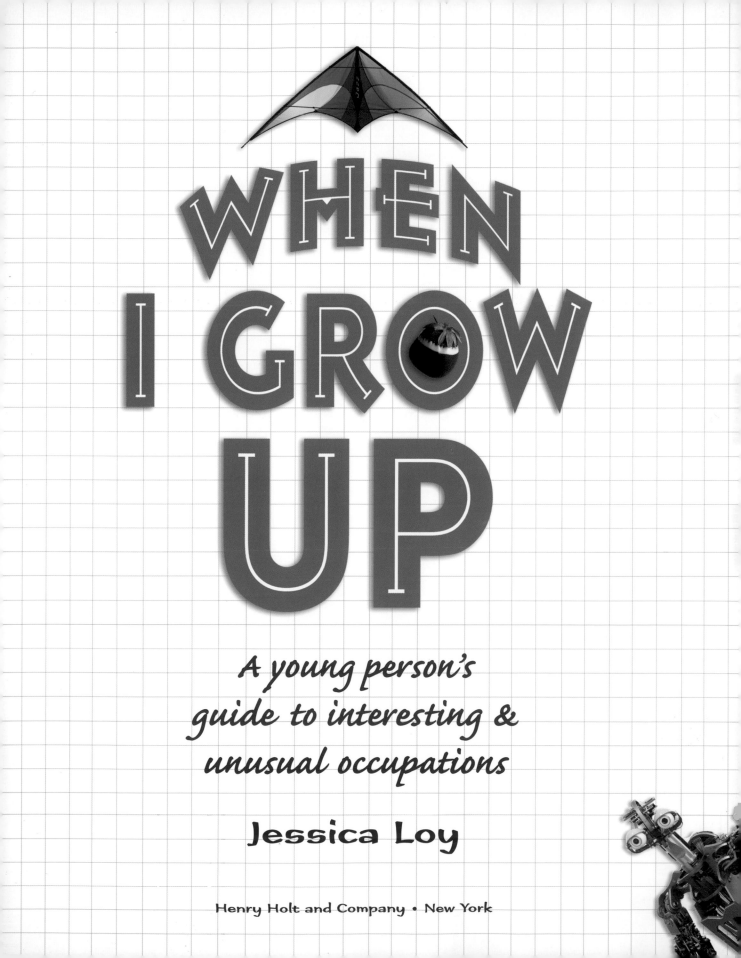

WHEN I GROW UP

A young person's
guide to interesting &
unusual occupations

Jessica Loy

Henry Holt and Company • New York

Introduction

How do we decide what we want to be when we grow up? We might get ideas from our families and teachers or from people we admire.

Inside you will find fourteen careers that began as dreams and have turned into lifelong pursuits. Many started as childhood interests. Maybe there is something you love to do that will someday become your career.

There are so many possibilities!

Contents

Jerry

Longhorn Beetle ▶

Comet Moth

Luna Moth Caterpillar

ENTOMOLOGIST
Jerry Dievendorf

The study of bugs and insects is called entomology. This is Jerry Dievendorf, and he's been crazy about entomology his whole life. In fact, his license plate reveals his favorite insect. "Insects are vital to the health and well-being of our planet," says Jerry.

Insects make up 80 percent of the species on the earth. It is estimated that 85 percent of insect species have never been collected or identified. But insect habitats diminish as the human population grows, making it even more important to find new species before they become extinct. Insects are also closely tied to human food crops and other food sources. Understanding insects, both the good and the bad, is important to our own survival.

Jerry has a collection of 200,000 insects from all over the world and has collected from Central America, Belize, Trinidad and Tobago, New Guinea, and around the United States. "You don't need to go anywhere special, though," says Jerry. As a kid, he would collect insects off truck radiators.

Jerry encourages drawing as a good way to focus students' attention on insect details.

Not all insects have common names. Those without are known by their scientific name, which describes them by genus and species.

Pearl Morpho

Harlequin Beetle

Sunset Moth
bottom side

Violin Beetle

Atlas Moth

This is a Malaise trap. Insects fly into the tent and up to the bottle, where they are collected.

Jerry raises moths and butterflies by enclosing caterpillars in netting he wraps around branches of trees that they like to eat. The caterpillars feed on the leaves, pupate, and hatch into adults in captivity.

There are many ways to entice insects into a trap. This bait trap uses fruit on a bottom tray. Insects always fly up to escape, so once they feed from the tray, they fly up into the netting and can't get out.

Ending the life of an insect and then mounting it the right way is critical to displaying every detail of the species. This allows entomologists to preserve and study the many varieties and discover new ones.

The hard part of the job is the responsibility of preserving insects properly so that their sacrifice is for a good cause.

Kids are naturally curious about insects. Jerry enjoys working with them to teach an appreciation and enthusiasm for science and nature.

Jerry uses a spreading board and pins to spread out the wings and legs of insects.

Once the insects dry, they will keep their shape and can be put in a display box.

Macrodontia cervicornis   *Morpho helena*   Rhinoceros Beetle   Sunset Moth
top side   Stag Beetle   *Morpho hecuba*   9

The Meade/Gilman Family

ALPACA FARMERS

Jupiter

Shaquille

Riverside Alpacas began in 1996 and is run by three generations of the Meade/Gilman family in Jordan, New York. Their job is to breed, raise, and care for alpacas, shear their wool, mill the wool into a variety of yarns, and create garments. They also mill wool sent to them by other alpaca farmers and attend county fairs, where they display their work, teach people about alpacas, and show their beautiful animals.

Alpacas originated in Chile, Peru, and Bolivia. These gentle animals are raised for their fine, soft wool, which can be woven into clothing. Alpaca wool is considered seven times stronger and more durable than sheep wool, and it is as soft as cashmere.

Keeping the alpacas healthy and happy is very important.

Before shearing

Chris runs the picker, which opens and loosens the alpaca fiber.

Next, the carder aligns the fibers.

The draw frame stretches the fibers to prepare them for spinning.

Alpacas come in twenty-two natural colors and are shorn once a year in the spring. Shearing is a job for the whole family because it takes many people to hold the animal, shear its coat, and trim around the face.

It's a lot of work to care for a herd of animals, but it is a job the family loves.

Fibers are spun into yarn on a computerized spinner.

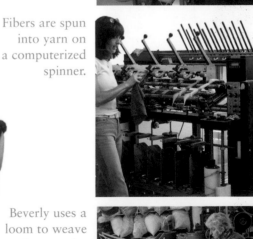

Beverly uses a loom to weave the yarn for a sweater.

After shearing

ARCHAEOLOGIST

Andrea Lain

Andrea Lain is an archaeologist at the New York State Museum in Albany. When she was eight years old, her great-grandmother gave her a set of books entitled *Wonders of the Past*. They were filled with pictures of old treasures from around the world. She decided almost at once that she would grow up to study times gone by.

"Archaeology is important because it is one of the only ways we have to learn about human existence in the past," says Andrea. "History books give a basic outline of what people did, but they mostly focus on the wealthy or famous. Objects found in archaeological excavations can tell us a lot about average people's lives. Food remains can show what they ate; a button or buckle can show what they wore; and pieces of broken dishes can tell us their economic status."

Excavating (or digging up) a site can be slow work, but finding bits and pieces of history is very exciting. It's important to record exactly where the objects were found, including their relationship to other objects and their depth in the soil.

After the pieces are brought back to the museum or lab, the real work begins—trying to understand what the objects mean.

A young volunteer helps Andrea pick through soil samples from a local excavation. So far, the sediments have revealed bones, glass, seashell fragments, burned charcoal, and a button.

Blue glass soda bottle

A blue transfer-printed
chamber pot fragment
from the 17th century
(an early form of the toilet)

A Native American
stone spear point

Glass buttons are
commonly found
at the sites of 19th-
century homes.

A comb made of
Bakelite, an early
form of plastic

A piece of the rim of a
prehistoric pottery vessel

42511

Identification numbers help
archaeologists find the artifacts
once they are stored in a collection.

One of Andrea's jobs is to make sure
everything at the museum is stored
properly so that other archaeologists can
continue to revisit and reinterpret artifacts
and their meanings far into the future.
The past can help us to understand the
future, but our understanding of the past
is always changing as archaeologists ask
new questions and find new answers.

Burned bone fragments
from a fireplace site

Clay pipe bowl and stem
from the 19th century

A deer jaw can tell about the diet of
16th-century Native Americans.

MASTER CHEESE MAKER

Jamie Miller

Jamie is holding cheese curds.

Meet Jamie Miller. He's the master cheese maker at Shelburne Farms in Shelburne, Vermont. He and his crew make premium cheddar cheeses, which age for six months to three years. They make an amazing 125,000 pounds of cheese a year by hand. It is sold to people all over the nation.

Jamie was trained as a restaurant cook. Wanting to try something different, he became an apprentice to a cheese maker. Now Jamie is responsible for carrying on the Shelburne Farms tradition of creating award-winning cheddar cheese.

Cheese making is physically demanding. This hands-on job starts at 7:30 A.M. with driving the tractor to the dairy to pick up fresh milk. The milk is then hauled back and pumped into the cheese-making vat.

Creating top-quality cheese means making sure all the steps are followed to perfection. Jamie says, "It's rewarding to put yourself completely into a product and be pleased with the results."

There is a lot of science used for cheese making. Good-tasting cheese requires the maker to continually check acidity levels and control the work of the bacteria cultures.

Jamie loves cheese. "Cheese is like superfood. It's all the good stuff in milk, concentrated." The basic ingredients are milk, bacteria (the friendly kind), rennet, and salt.

Visitors to Shelburne Farms can watch the step-by-step process through a viewing window in the Farm Barn.

1. The cheese process begins with milk from Shelburne Farms' very own brown Swiss cows. The cheese makers collect the milk fresh every morning from the dairy.

2. A bacterial culture is stirred into warm milk to start the fermenting process. An hour later, rennet, an enzyme, is added to thicken the mixture.

3. The coagulated milk is cut. This cutting results in the separation of milk into curds (solids) and whey (liquids).

4. The whey is drained and used to fertilize the farm fields.

◄ 5. Stacking the curds helps drain the moisture and gives the bacteria time to multiply. This is called "cheddaring."

◄ 6. When Jamie determines that the acidity level is right, he mills the slabs into "fingers."

7. Salt is mixed into the cheese fingers to stop the bacteria from growing.

8. The fingers are poured into molds called hoops and pressed overnight.

9. The next day, solid cheese blocks are removed and wrapped up to begin the aging process.

10. Mark slices and weighs aged cheese ready to be packaged.

11. The packaged cheese is labeled.

◄ 12. The cheese is ready to be sold.

Research Biologist

Nafeeza Hafeez

Nafeeza Hafeez is a cell biologist and researcher at Infinity Pharmaceuticals in Cambridge, Massachusetts, where she is working to find a cure for a variety of cancers.

Nafeeza works with cells using a special vented cell culture hood to make sure she doesn't contaminate them. She also wears gloves and goggles.

Nafeeza is studying a protein called Bc12 that's present in all cells but is especially abundant in cancer cells. Bc12 prevents cancer cells from dying. If Nafeeza can find a way to reduce Bc12 in a cancer cell, then the cancer cells might be able to be killed.

Nafeeza works in a team made up of chemists who create the molecules that will reduce the protein, biochemists who look for molecule interactions with the protein, cell biologists who look at the effects of the molecules on the protein in cancer cells, and pharmacologists (scientists who study how

Nafeeza uses a pipette to transfer liquid from one container to another.

pipette ▶

drugs work) who look at the effects of the molecule in test subjects.

Nafeeza enjoys the challenges. Sometimes she finds successful solutions, but sometimes she hits dead ends. That's the gamble of research, but it's always intriguing.

"There is no better feeling," says Nafeeza, "than finding a cure for an ailment or helping to improve someone's life." Sometimes people even send her thank-you notes.

Cells are kept in an incubator that mimics their normal growth environment.

This is a 96-well plate for growing cells. Color solution is added to determine whether cells are alive or dead. Pink represents living cells. Blue represents dead cells. This is how researchers can tell if the cancer cells have been killed.

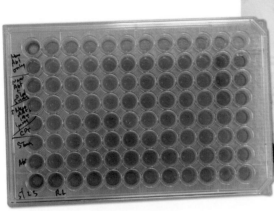

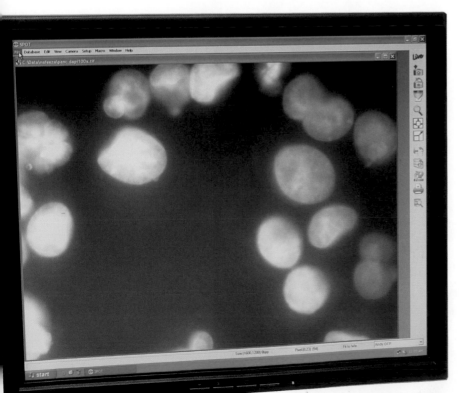

▲ Individual cells are not visible to the human eye, therefore they can only be viewed when magnified under a microscope.

◄ Computer images give an even closer view of individual cells.

Peter Seungtaek Lee

GAME DESIGNER

Peter Seungtaek Lee has been designing digital and nondigital games for eight years, but he's been an avid game player all his life. As cofounder and president of Gamelab in New York City, he spends every day creating new games for kids and grown-ups.

All the game characters start as simple pencil drawings before they are moved into the computer environment.

Diner Dash is one of Gamelab's most popular games.

The inspiration for creating games often comes from ▶ playing games, and Gamelab keeps stacks of them.

Peter was educated both as a visual artist and as a programmer, but he says his love of games was the best training of all. "Creating a game requires many people with different skills. You need programmers, writers, project managers, designers, illustrators, and sound designers." These skills are used to create the story-boards, background art, character art, texture design, animation, 3-D modeling, and all the other complex elements that make up a digital game.

How is a game built? First someone comes up with an idea. Then a playable prototype is created, which begins to test the basic interaction and game logic to see if the game is fun. Once the game tests positively, full production begins by bringing in visual and audio elements. Throughout the process, people play-test the game many times. The hardest part is the problem-solving.

Peter admits, "The fun part of playing a game comes after long days of work. Making a game is very challenging, but it is also very satisfying."

The games Gamelab creates are played online or distributed over the Internet.

Peter's favorite game that he developed is *Diner Dash*. It's about a waitress trying to keep her customers happy. Gamelab also creates many games for the LEGO Web site.

"I love to hear how much people enjoy playing the games I helped to create."

Each member of the team works on a different aspect of a project.

Team meetings are an important part of idea development and troubleshooting.

In a studio everyone contributes their expertise to solve a problem.

CHOCOLATIER

Lissa D'Aquanni

"**W**hen I was young, my aunt Loretta had a chocolate shop. I remember it was a magical place . . . a place I loved to visit," says Lissa D'Aquanni. Years later Lissa began experimenting with making her own chocolate and in 1998 started The Chocolate Gecko—with Aunt Loretta's blessing.

The best part of making chocolate, says Lissa, "is creating something special for people who are going through a difficult period. It is said that chocolate has medicinal properties and that, combined with the love that we put into our creations, helps to sweeten even the most bitter times." Lissa makes chocolates for happy times, too, such as weddings, anniversaries, birthdays, and other special occasions.

The secret to her gourmet creations is play. Lissa starts by combining ingredients from favorite recipes until she finds a tasty new treat. Customer favorites are the Galapagos Turtles, made with maple syrup caramel, and her fruits, hand-dipped in white and dark chocolate.

Lissa tops the caramel base of her Galapagos Turtles with milk chocolate.
▼

Tropical Storm Truffle

Galapagos Turtle

Helderberg Nugget

Chocolate Butterfly

Hand-dipped Strawberries

Komodo Crunch

Dark Chocolate Brick

Dark Chocolate Love Birds

Lissa says the hardest part of the job is keeping up with the demand of big orders. She once had to make 2,500 dipped strawberries for the governor's inauguration to be delivered the morning of January 1. It was a long New Year's Eve!

Lissa takes orders through her Web site, but she prefers when people come into the shop so she can meet them. Lissa likes to see people enjoying her treats.

The final touch on the Galapagos Turtles is a lovely sugar flower.

The Komodo Crunch is toffee finished with a chocolate dip and a roll in nuts.

Granola is mixed with dried fruit, nuts, and dark chocolate for the Helderberg Nugget.

The nuggets are made by scooping spoonfuls into small cups.

Percussionist

Donald Knaack

Donald Knaack is the Junkman. He is an accomplished percussionist who started his career in the Louisville Orchestra. One year every orchestra member needed to play a small scrap of metal for a contemporary piece.

Donald's job was to go to the junkyard and get the necessary metal. "It was my first time in a junkyard, and I was overwhelmed by the amazing variety of sounds that junk materials possessed." Donald found what he needed for the orchestra and a carload of junk for himself. He has been collecting and using junk to compose and perform music ever since—bringing an environmental theme to his work and to the world.

All Donald's instruments have names. This one is called the Rasping Rack.

What kind of junk does Donald look for? "Unusual sounds—beautiful sounds like bells, ugly sounds like thunder, strange sounds like rasping a metal staircase." He finds it in all types of wood, metal, plastic, paper, glass, and cardboard. Then Donald puts the junk together to create an instrument that is both fun to play and to watch.

One of the most important parts of building a community play station is bringing the community together to play their creation. Everyone joins in.

The Junkman tours all over the world. He has composed music for Twyla Tharp and the American Ballet Theatre, and performed in schools, colleges, universities, and big events such as Boston's First Night celebration.

Donald spends time at schools as a visiting artist, teaching kids about rhythm and recycling while helping them build their own Junk Music play station. The play station becomes a permanent part of their school, to be enjoyed for years to come.

The newly installed play station at Cambridge Elementary School in Vermont

Donald works with kids at their school to assemble their own community play station.

Linda Greenlaw
Lobsterman

Linda Greenlaw has been fishing most of her life. She began her career fishing for swordfish and eventually became captain of her own boat. After an adventurous seventeen years, she decided to fish closer to home in Isle au Haut, Maine. Now she catches lobster off the coast of the island. Her boat, the *Mattie Belle*, is named after her grandmother.

The lobster season runs from May to December. When the weather gets cold, the lobster move to deeper water and can no longer be caught. During the winter months, Linda prepares her gear and paints her buoys for the next season. "This is the hardest part of the job," says Linda, "because it's a lot of tedious work without the fun of being on the water."

Lobstering begins early in the morning. Linda maneuvers up to her first buoy and catches it using a hook called a gaff.

Linda throws back a crab, which is a common catch in the traps.

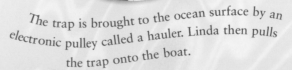

The trap is brought to the ocean surface by an electronic pulley called a hauler. Linda then pulls the trap onto the boat.

Each lobster is measured using a special gauge. If the lobster is too small, it must be thrown back to grow, and if it is too big, it is thrown back to reproduce. Females with eggs are also thrown back. These important precautions help to ensure the future of lobsters and lobster fishing. ▶

After stopping at the community bait house, Linda fills her bait bags.

The bait bag is filled with herring to lure the lobster into the traps.
▼

◀ The lobster is turned over to determine whether it is a female and if she has eggs.

Buoys float on the water attached with rope to the lobster trap on the bottom of the ocean. Lobster fishermen have their own color and pattern of buoy to identify their gear. Linda chose orange because it stands out in ◀ the fog.

banding

After she baits the trap, it is ready to go back into the sea.

Once lobsters are caught, bands are put around their claws so that they won't hurt the fisherman or each other.

25

Guitar Makers

Julius and Steve love to play and build guitars. They produce only twenty guitars a year because each one must be perfect. Steve says the work is enjoyable since he is always doing something different, and Julius is proud of the unique sound people have come to expect from his instruments.

"Building instruments is a wonderful outlet for creativity. You start with a pile of wood and end up with a beautiful tool for making music—one that will give joy to people for generations to come," says Steve. But making guitars is also physically demanding work. You have to love what you do and work hard for many years to become a successful builder.

Guitar making requires excellent woodworking skills, problem solving, math and science, curiosity, patience, and a musical background. The best way to learn is by working as an apprentice with an expert builder.

Guitars are made from a variety of woods such as spruce, maple, mahogany, and rosewood. What makes a great instrument? The careful selection of wood and its processing to create the guitar parts. The soundboard (large top part of the guitar) is critical because it's responsible for the tone of the instrument.

Julius handles all the design and development. Steve's job is to assist Julius in the construction. This can include the body and neck, decoration, and inlay work. Selecting materials, voicing the instruments, and the critical finish work is what makes the instrument play properly.

Because the guitars are custom built, most are bought by collectors and professional musicians who have the skill to bring out the best in a great guitar.

Julius Borges ▸

Steve Spodaryk ▸

26

1. Lots of time is spent cutting and shaping wood on power saws. Steve is cutting braces for a new guitar.

2. Bending wood in a mold requires just the right amount of heat and pressure to give the guitar its distinctive shape.

3. The guitar begins to take shape.

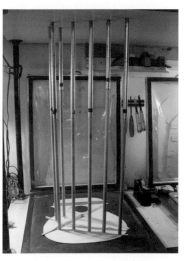

4. A traditional method of gluing braces to the inside of a guitar, and using spring rods for pressure, dates as far back as the ancient Egyptians.

5. Steve shows what the inside of a guitar looks like. The patterned pieces of wood are braces and give a guitar its distinctive sound.

6. The inlay is a detail that adds beauty to the guitar.

7. After being stained and sprayed with varnish, guitars are hung up to dry.

8. Julius carefully polishes a finished guitar.

Kite Designer

Mark Reed

Mark Reed is the owner and designer of Prism Designs. He creates single-line and two-line sport kites for people addicted to flying kites. Mark spent his early years working to understand the physics of sport kites, and he continues to refine his designs with each new project.

"I have always been a builder of things and for most of my childhood fancied myself either an inventor or a mad scientist," says Mark. "When I discovered stunt kites, the sport had barely gotten off the ground. It was exciting to experiment with design ideas knowing that I was making things that had never been built before."

Two-line sport kites are not the same as traditional kites, which go up on one string and stay in one part of the sky. Two-line sport kites are maneuverable, can fly up to speeds of 100 miles per hour, and do cartwheels, somersaults, and backflips.

Quantum
The seven-foot wingspan is exciting yet stable for a first-time flyer.

Prism Designs kites are built by hand:
1. Shapes are cut out of special fabric and pieced together with double-sided tape.
2. The pieces are sewn together. Each style of kite uses a different combination of fabrics and tension.
3. Finally, the frame is added and tested for balance and precision.

28

Hypnotist
This kite does all the latest freestyle tricks.

Stylus P.1
This kite has no frame, but a strong wind gives it a powerful pull.

Triad
Prism's only single-line box kite can fly like a traditional kite or dance in the wind.

Catalyst
A simple and rugged entry-level kite

Elixir
Considered one of the Prism elite kites

Prism makes specialized kites for tricks, for speed, for pulling, for light winds, strong winds, and for indoors. The indoor kite is so light, it takes very little air movement to get it airborne.

Serious kite enthusiasts usually can't settle for just one of these kites; they own a different style for each kind of flying condition.

Nexus
Small and packable, great kite for traveling

Nexus 5-Stack
A great way to impress a crowd

photo by Mark Reed

Kim Levin

Pet Photographer

Kim Levin is a pet photographer in Little Silver, New Jersey. She often works with dogs and cats but has been assigned to photograph horses, parrots, guinea pigs, and rabbits. She never says no to a pet.

Kim's clients are often pet owners looking for a special portrait, but she also does work for business clients such as the American Kennel Club and Animal Planet. When Kim gets an assignment, she travels to the pet because home is where the animal will be most comfortable. She usually needs two hours to take enough pictures to capture her subject's personality. How does she get a pet's cooperation? "I rely on treats, playing my harmonica, and lots of love." Kim likes to shoot black-and-white photographs because of their timeless quality. Around the holidays, clients ask for more color images. Her favorite experiences—photographing the NYPD K-9 Unit at Ground Zero in the aftermath of September 11. And photographing television's Lassie in 1998.

Kim highlights the pictures on the contact sheets that she thinks will make the best photographic portrait. She is looking for more than just a pretty face. She wants to capture a pet's personality.

Richard Finkelstein
SET DESIGNER

Richard Finkelstein has loved to build since he was four years old. During high school he focused that interest by designing and acting in school theater productions. Now he lives in Harrisonburg, Virginia, and designs theater sets around the country.

A career in set design usually begins with a background in the performing or fine arts along with an apprenticeship with a seasoned designer. It's also very important to have good drawing skills.

Richard enjoys the research process involved in set design. He finds learning about other time periods and cultures fascinating, and this helps him turn the blank stage into a whole new world.

A set requires lots of paint to create the illusion of surfaces such as marble, brick, and tiles, but a set is also about sculpture. It's the job of the designer to make sure that the actors can move around the set and that the audience can easily see them.

Richard has designed many theater sets and each one enables him to challenge his imagination.

Design drawings and plans get worked out on the computer.

A brick wall starts with a plastic facade that is painted to create the illusion of a brick building.

The Lost Boys' hideaway, designed for *Peter Pan*

But designers can't do it alone. They need to work well with others because it takes many people to build, paint, and outfit the sets Richard designs.

Ultimately when the curtain rises Richard's work is judged by the critics, and the audience. But that's part of the job, and like any artist, he has learned to take it in stride.

The color computer sketch in the upper right corner was the starting point for the finished set of *A Tale of Cinderella.*

A production of *The Wizard of Oz* presented by the New York State Theatre Institute, where Richard designs many shows

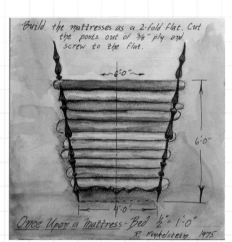

Build the mattresses as a 2-fold flat. Cut the posts out of 3/8" ply and screw to the flat.

6'0"

6'0"

4'0"

Once Upon a Mattress – Bed 1/2" = 1'0"
R. Finkelstein 1975

A drawing for *Once Upon a Mattress* shows carpenters and painters exactly what the designer wants.

◄ Richard takes a moment to speak with one of the actors while overseeing work on the set of *Man of La Mancha.* So far, only the brick wall is in place.

Aaron Edsinger

ROBOTICS ENGINEER

This is Aaron Edsinger. He designs and builds robots. He's been building all his life, and his childhood idol was the inventor Thomas Edison. Now Aaron puts his skills to work building complex robots for scientific research at the Massachusetts Institute of Technology in Cambridge, Massachusetts.

Robot design begins with renderings like these of Domo's ◀ head and hand. ▼

Aaron's current robot is Domo. Domo helps Aaron study how the human mind works. By using a robot, he can safely test ideas about brain function.

So far, Aaron has built three research robots and five robot sculptures for entertainment. Depending on the complexity, a robot can take from three days to three years to build.

Robots are exciting because they have the potential to improve lives, entertain, and help explore the world. They are used just about everywhere—in research, space travel, games, and surgery.

Aaron says the most rewarding part of his job is watching the robot come alive. "When you see it moving around and forget for a minute that it's just a bunch of motors and gears, that's amazing." The only frustrating part is that robots can break down.

Soldering electronic components

Along with designing the robot, Aaron is responsible for building it. He uses the machine shop to cut steel parts and file cylinders. He also creates the circuitry and welds the components together. Designing robots takes both imagination and persistence to solve complex problems.

Aaron puts in around ten hours a day at his job. He says that engineering and computer science are important skills for a career in building robots.

Cutting a round metal piece on the lathe creates a part for an elbow joint.

In the shop, the machines allow Aaron to transform his computer designs into actual robot parts.

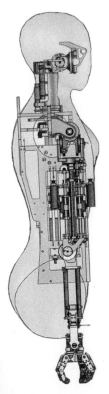

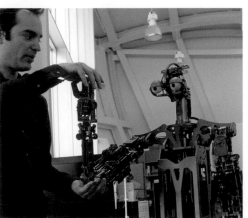

Aaron shows how Domo's hand works to grasp things.

◀ The robot is designed to simulate the head, torso, arms, and hands of a human, as shown in this drawing.

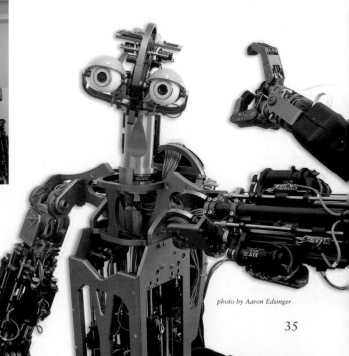

photo by Aaron Edsinger

Resources

Jerry Dievendorf
Field Research and Scientific Studies
(FRASS)
19 Rose Court
Delmar, New York 12054

A+ Alpaca Fiber Mill
and Riverside Alpacas
6781 River Road
Jordan, New York 13080
315.689.1649
www.riversidealpacas.com

New York State Museum
Cultural Education Center
Albany, New York
www.nysm.nysed.gov

Shelburne Farms
1611 Harbor Road
Shelburne, Vermont 05482
802.985.8686
www.shelburnefarms.org

Nafeeza Hafeez
Infinity Pharmaceuticals
780 Memorial Drive
Cambridge, Massachusetts 02139
617.453.1000
www.ipi.com

Peter Seungtaek Lee
Gamelab
368 Broadway #210
New York, New York 10013
646.827.6644
www.gamelab.com

The Chocolate Gecko
540 Delaware Avenue
Albany, New York 12209
518.436.0866
www.chocolategecko.com

The Junkman
The Moo Group
P.O. Box 2074
Manchester, Vermont 05255
www.junkmusic.org

Linda Greenlaw
www.fishingwithlinda.net

Borges Guitars
410 Great Road, A-2
Littleton, Massachusetts 01460
www.borgesguitars.com

Prism Designs, Inc.
4214 24th Avenue West
Seattle, Washington 98199
206.547.1100
www.prismkites.com

Kim Levin
Bark & Smile Pet Portraits
www.barkandsmile.com

Richard Finkelstein
630 Stonewall Drive
Harrisonburg, Virginia 22801
www.rfdesigns.org

Aaron Edsinger
Humanoid Robotics Group
MIT Computer Science and
Artificial Intelligence Laboratory
Cambridge, Massachusetts 02139
www.csail.mit.edu/~edsinger

Below is a list of summer camps that offer an opportunity for kids to explore potential career paths. This represents only a small number of camps that offer specialized learning and provide a wonderful chance for kids to explore their interests and their future.

Camp Kennedy Space Center
Kids Space Program Summer Camps
Ages 8–14
www.kennedyspacecenter.com
/educatorsParents/camp.asp

Dartmouth Summer Camp
Health Careers Camp
Grades 10–12
dms.dartmouth.edu/camp/faq

Fort Worth Zoo
Summer Career Camps
Grades 9–12
www.fortworthzoo.com/school/
summer_career.html

Frenchwoods Festival
of the Performing Arts
Tech Theater Camp
Ages 10–15
www.frenchwoods.com

Idaho POST Academy
Law Enforcement Career Camp
www.idaho-post.org/Career_Camp/
careercamp.html

Kentucky Humane Society
Career Discovery Camp
Ages 13–16
www.kyhumane.org

Kids Culinary Camp of Vermont
Ages 7 and up
kidssummercampforcooking.com

National Computer Camps
www.nccamp.com

National Geographic Photo Camp
Ages 12–20
www.nationalgeographic.com/
photocamp

New York Summer Music Festival
Ages 10–25
www.nysmf.org/101-intro.html

Organization of Black Airline Pilots
Aviation Camp
Ages 13–18
www.obap.org

Salty Dog Camps
Fishing, First Mate and Boat
Building Camps
Ages 10–15
www.saltydogcamps.com

SeaWorld
Career Discovery Camps
Grades 10–12
www.buschgardens.org

Union College Robot Camp
Grades 7–12
www.union.edu/robotcamp

These listings are not an endorsement. Any new camp experience should be researched with care.